Monthly
Budget Planner

This book belongs to

....

....

Beware of little expenses;
a small leak will sink a great ship.
- Benjamin Franklin

Monthly BUDGET

Month :

Budget :

Expenses

	Income		
Source1			
Source2			
Other Income			
TOTAL INCOME			

No.	Bill	Date	Amount	Paid
	TOTAL EXPENSES			

Monthly BUDGET

No.	Date	Other Expenses	Amount
		TOTAL OTHER EXPENSE	

Notes

TOTAL INCOME

TOTAL EXPENSES

DIFFERENCE

Weekly Expense Tracker

Month : _____ **Week of :** _____ **Budget :** _____

Mon

Description	Amount
TOTAL	

Tue

Description	Amount
TOTAL	

Wed

Description	Amount
TOTAL	

Thu

Description	Amount
TOTAL	

Weekly Expense Tracker

Total expenses :

Balance :

Fri

Description	Amount
TOTAL	

Sat

Description	Amount
TOTAL	

Sun

Description	Amount
TOTAL	

Notes

Weekly Expense Tracker

Month :   **Week of :**   **Budget :**

Mon

Description	Amount
TOTAL	

Tue

Description	Amount
TOTAL	

Wed

Description	Amount
TOTAL	

Thu

Description	Amount
TOTAL	

Weekly Expense Tracker

Total expenses :

Balance :

Fri

Description	Amount
TOTAL	

Sat

Description	Amount
TOTAL	

Sun

Description	Amount
TOTAL	

Notes

Weekly Expense Tracker

Month : **Week of :** **Budget :**

Mon

Description	Amount
TOTAL	

Tue

Description	Amount
TOTAL	

Wed

Description	Amount
TOTAL	

Thu

Description	Amount
TOTAL	

Weekly Expense Tracker

Total expenses :

Balance :

Fri

Description	Amount
TOTAL	

Sat

Description	Amount
TOTAL	

Sun

Description	Amount
TOTAL	

Notes

Weekly Expense Tracker

Month : _____   **Week of :** _____   **Budget :** _____

Mon

Description	Amount
TOTAL	

Tue

Description	Amount
TOTAL	

Wed

Description	Amount
TOTAL	

Thu

Description	Amount
TOTAL	

Weekly Expense Tracker

Total expenses :

Balance :

Fri

Description	Amount
TOTAL	

Sat

Description	Amount
TOTAL	

Sun

Description	Amount
TOTAL	

Notes

Weekly Expense Tracker

Month : **Week of :** **Budget :**

Mon

Description	Amount
TOTAL	

Tue

Description	Amount
TOTAL	

Wed

Description	Amount
TOTAL	

Thu

Description	Amount
TOTAL	

Weekly Expense Tracker

Total expenses :

Balance :

Fri

Description	Amount
TOTAL	

Sat

Description	Amount
TOTAL	

Sun

Description	Amount
TOTAL	

Notes

Monthly BUDGET

Month :

Budget :

Expenses

	Income		
Source1		
Source2		
Other Income		
TOTAL INCOME			

No.	Bill	Date	Amount	Paid
		TOTAL EXPENSES		

Monthly BUDGET

No.	Date	Other Expenses	Amount
		TOTAL OTHER EXPENSE	

Notes

TOTAL INCOME

TOTAL EXPENSES

DIFFERENCE

Weekly Expense Tracker

Month : _____   **Week of :** _____   **Budget :** _____

Mon

Description	Amount
TOTAL	

Tue

Description	Amount
TOTAL	

Wed

Description	Amount
TOTAL	

Thu

Description	Amount
TOTAL	

Weekly Expense Tracker

Total expenses :

Balance :

Fri

Description	Amount
TOTAL	

Sat

Description	Amount
TOTAL	

Sun

Description	Amount
TOTAL	

Notes

Weekly Expense Tracker

Month : **Week of :** **Budget :**

Mon

Description	Amount
TOTAL	

Tue

Description	Amount
TOTAL	

Wed

Description	Amount
TOTAL	

Thu

Description	Amount
TOTAL	

Weekly Expense Tracker

Total expenses :

Balance :

Fri

Description	Amount
TOTAL	

Sat

Description	Amount
TOTAL	

Sun

Description	Amount
TOTAL	

Notes

Weekly Expense Tracker

Month : _____   **Week of :** _____   **Budget :** _____

Mon

Description	Amount
TOTAL	

Tue

Description	Amount
TOTAL	

Wed

Description	Amount
TOTAL	

Thu

Description	Amount
TOTAL	

Weekly Expense Tracker

Total expenses :

Balance :

Fri

Description	Amount
TOTAL	

Sat

Description	Amount
TOTAL	

Sun

Description	Amount
TOTAL	

Notes

Weekly Expense Tracker

Month :   **Week of :**   **Budget :**

Mon

Description	Amount
TOTAL	

Tue

Description	Amount
TOTAL	

Wed

Description	Amount
TOTAL	

Thu

Description	Amount
TOTAL	

Weekly Expense Tracker

Total expenses :

Balance :

Fri

Description	Amount
TOTAL	

Sat

Description	Amount
TOTAL	

Sun

Description	Amount
TOTAL	

Notes

Weekly Expense Tracker

Month : _____   **Week of :** _____   **Budget :** _____

Mon

Description	Amount
TOTAL	

Tue

Description	Amount
TOTAL	

Wed

Description	Amount
TOTAL	

Thu

Description	Amount
TOTAL	

Weekly Expense Tracker

Total expenses :

Balance :

Fri

Description	Amount
TOTAL	

Sat

Description	Amount
TOTAL	

Sun

Description	Amount
TOTAL	

Notes

Monthly BUDGET

Month :

Budget :

Expenses

Income		
Source1		
Source2		
Other Income		
TOTAL INCOME		

No.	Bill	Date	Amount	Paid
		TOTAL EXPENSES		

Monthly BUDGET

No.	Date	Other Expenses	Amount
		TOTAL OTHER EXPENSE	

Notes

TOTAL INCOME

TOTAL EXPENSES

DIFFERENCE

Weekly Expense Tracker

Month : **Week of :** **Budget :**

Mon

Description	Amount
TOTAL	

Tue

Description	Amount
TOTAL	

Wed

Description	Amount
TOTAL	

Thu

Description	Amount
TOTAL	

Weekly Expense Tracker

Total expenses :

Balance :

Fri

Description	Amount
TOTAL	

Sat

Description	Amount
TOTAL	

Sun

Description	Amount
TOTAL	

Notes

Weekly Expense Tracker

Month :   **Week of :**   **Budget :**

Mon

Description	Amount
TOTAL	

Tue

Description	Amount
TOTAL	

Wed

Description	Amount
TOTAL	

Thu

Description	Amount
TOTAL	

Weekly Expense Tracker

Total expenses :

Balance :

Fri

Description	Amount
TOTAL	

Sat

Description	Amount
TOTAL	

Sun

Description	Amount
TOTAL	

Notes

Weekly Expense Tracker

Month : **Week of :** **Budget :**

Mon

Description	Amount
TOTAL	

Tue

Description	Amount
TOTAL	

Wed

Description	Amount
TOTAL	

Thu

Description	Amount
TOTAL	

Weekly Expense Tracker

Total expenses :

Balance :

Fri

Description	Amount
TOTAL	

Sat

Description	Amount
TOTAL	

Sun

Description	Amount
TOTAL	

Notes

Weekly Expense Tracker

Month :   **Week of :**   **Budget :**

Mon

Description	Amount
TOTAL	

Tue

Description	Amount
TOTAL	

Wed

Description	Amount
TOTAL	

Thu

Description	Amount
TOTAL	

Weekly Expense Tracker

Total expenses :

Balance :

Fri

Description	Amount
TOTAL	

Sat

Description	Amount
TOTAL	

Sun

Description	Amount
TOTAL	

Notes

Weekly Expense Tracker

Month : _____   **Week of :** _____   **Budget :** _____

Mon

Description	Amount
TOTAL	

Tue

Description	Amount
TOTAL	

Wed

Description	Amount
TOTAL	

Thu

Description	Amount
TOTAL	

Weekly Expense Tracker

Total expenses :

Balance :

Fri

Description	Amount
TOTAL	

Sat

Description	Amount
TOTAL	

Sun

Description	Amount
TOTAL	

Notes

Monthly BUDGET

Month :

Budget :

Expenses

Income		
Source1		
Source2		
Other Income		
TOTAL INCOME		

No.	Bill	Date	Amount	Paid
	TOTAL EXPENSES			

Monthly BUDGET

No.	Date	Other Expenses	Amount
		TOTAL OTHER EXPENSE	

Notes
....
....
....
....
....

TOTAL INCOME

TOTAL EXPENSES

DIFFERENCE

Weekly Expense Tracker

Month : **Week of :** **Budget :**

Mon

Description	Amount
TOTAL	

Tue

Description	Amount
TOTAL	

Wed

Description	Amount
TOTAL	

Thu

Description	Amount
TOTAL	

Weekly Expense Tracker

Total expenses :

Balance :

Fri

Description	Amount
TOTAL	

Sat

Description	Amount
TOTAL	

Sun

Description	Amount
TOTAL	

Notes

Weekly Expense Tracker

Month : **Week of :** **Budget :**

Mon

Description	Amount
TOTAL	

Tue

Description	Amount
TOTAL	

Wed

Description	Amount
TOTAL	

Thu

Description	Amount
TOTAL	

Weekly Expense Tracker

Total expenses :

Balance :

Fri

Description	Amount
TOTAL	

Sat

Description	Amount
TOTAL	

Sun

Description	Amount
TOTAL	

Notes

Weekly Expense Tracker

Month :   **Week of :**   **Budget :**

Mon

Description	Amount
TOTAL	

Tue

Description	Amount
TOTAL	

Wed

Description	Amount
TOTAL	

Thu

Description	Amount
TOTAL	

Weekly Expense Tracker

Total expenses : _____

Balance : _____

Fri

Description	Amount
TOTAL	

Sat

Description	Amount
TOTAL	

Sun

Description	Amount
TOTAL	

Notes

Weekly Expense Tracker

Month : _____   **Week of :** _____   **Budget :** _____

Mon

Description	Amount
TOTAL	

Tue

Description	Amount
TOTAL	

Wed

Description	Amount
TOTAL	

Thu

Description	Amount
TOTAL	

Weekly Expense Tracker

Total expenses :

Balance :

Fri

Description	Amount
TOTAL	

Sat

Description	Amount
TOTAL	

Sun

Description	Amount
TOTAL	

Notes

Weekly Expense Tracker

Month : **Week of :** **Budget :**

Mon

Description	Amount
TOTAL	

Tue

Description	Amount
TOTAL	

Wed

Description	Amount
TOTAL	

Thu

Description	Amount
TOTAL	

Weekly Expense Tracker

Total expenses :

Balance :

Fri

Description	Amount
TOTAL	

Sat

Description	Amount
TOTAL	

Sun

Description	Amount
TOTAL	

Notes

Monthly BUDGET

Month :

Budget :

Expenses

Income		
Source1		
Source2		
Other Income		
TOTAL INCOME		

No.	Bill	Date	Amount	Paid
		TOTAL EXPENSES		

Monthly BUDGET

No.	Date	Other Expenses	Amount
		TOTAL OTHER EXPENSE	

Notes

TOTAL INCOME

TOTAL EXPENSES

DIFFERENCE

Weekly Expense Tracker

Month :   **Week of :**   **Budget :**

Mon

Description	Amount
TOTAL	

Tue

Description	Amount
TOTAL	

Wed

Description	Amount
TOTAL	

Thu

Description	Amount
TOTAL	

Weekly Expense Tracker

Total expenses :

Balance :

Fri

Description	Amount
TOTAL	

Sat

Description	Amount
TOTAL	

Sun

Description	Amount
TOTAL	

Notes

Weekly Expense Tracker

Month : **Week of :** **Budget :**

Mon

Description	Amount
	TOTAL

Tue

Description	Amount
	TOTAL

Wed

Description	Amount
	TOTAL

Thu

Description	Amount
	TOTAL

Weekly Expense Tracker

Total expenses :

Balance :

Fri

Description	Amount
TOTAL	

Sat

Description	Amount
TOTAL	

Sun

Description	Amount
TOTAL	

Notes

Weekly Expense Tracker

Month : **Week of :** **Budget :**

Mon

Description	Amount
TOTAL	

Tue

Description	Amount
TOTAL	

Wed

Description	Amount
TOTAL	

Thu

Description	Amount
TOTAL	

Weekly Expense Tracker

Total expenses :

Balance :

Fri

Description	Amount
TOTAL	

Sat

Description	Amount
TOTAL	

Sun

Description	Amount
TOTAL	

Notes

Weekly Expense Tracker

Month :   **Week of :**   **Budget :**

Mon

Description	Amount
TOTAL	

Tue

Description	Amount
TOTAL	

Wed

Description	Amount
TOTAL	

Thu

Description	Amount
TOTAL	

Weekly Expense Tracker

Total expenses :

Balance :

Fri

Description	Amount
TOTAL	

Sat

Description	Amount
TOTAL	

Sun

Description	Amount
TOTAL	

Notes

Weekly Expense Tracker

Month :   **Week of :**   **Budget :**

Mon

Description	Amount
TOTAL	

Tue

Description	Amount
TOTAL	

Wed

Description	Amount
TOTAL	

Thu

Description	Amount
TOTAL	

Weekly Expense Tracker

Total expenses :

Balance :

Fri

Description	Amount
TOTAL	

Sat

Description	Amount
TOTAL	

Sun

Description	Amount
TOTAL	

Notes

Monthly BUDGET

Month :

Budget :

Expenses

Income		
Source1		
Source2		
Other Income		
TOTAL INCOME		

No.	Bill	Date	Amount	Paid
		TOTAL EXPENSES		

Monthly BUDGET

No.	Date	Other Expenses	Amount
		TOTAL OTHER EXPENSE	

Notes

TOTAL INCOME

TOTAL EXPENSES

DIFFERENCE

Weekly Expense Tracker

Month :   **Week of :**   **Budget :**

Mon

Description	Amount
TOTAL	

Tue

Description	Amount
TOTAL	

Wed

Description	Amount
TOTAL	

Thu

Description	Amount
TOTAL	

Weekly Expense Tracker

Total expenses :

Balance :

Fri

Description	Amount
TOTAL	

Sat

Description	Amount
TOTAL	

Sun

Description	Amount
TOTAL	

Notes

Weekly Expense Tracker

Month :   **Week of :**   **Budget :**

Mon

Description	Amount
TOTAL	

Tue

Description	Amount
TOTAL	

Wed

Description	Amount
TOTAL	

Thu

Description	Amount
TOTAL	

Weekly Expense Tracker

Total expenses :

Balance :

Fri

Description	Amount
TOTAL	

Sat

Description	Amount
TOTAL	

Sun

Description	Amount
TOTAL	

Notes

Weekly Expense Tracker

Month : _____   **Week of :** _____   **Budget :** _____

Mon

Description	Amount
TOTAL	

Tue

Description	Amount
TOTAL	

Wed

Description	Amount
TOTAL	

Thu

Description	Amount
TOTAL	

Weekly Expense Tracker

Total expenses :

Balance :

Fri

Description	Amount
TOTAL	

Sat

Description	Amount
TOTAL	

Sun

Description	Amount
TOTAL	

Notes

Weekly Expense Tracker

Month : **Week of :** **Budget :**

Mon

Description	Amount
TOTAL	

Tue

Description	Amount
TOTAL	

Wed

Description	Amount
TOTAL	

Thu

Description	Amount
TOTAL	

Weekly Expense Tracker

Total expenses :

Balance :

Fri

Description	Amount
TOTAL	

Sat

Description	Amount
TOTAL	

Sun

Description	Amount
TOTAL	

Notes

Weekly Expense Tracker

Month : _____ **Week of :** _____ **Budget :** _____

Mon

Description	Amount
TOTAL	

Tue

Description	Amount
TOTAL	

Wed

Description	Amount
TOTAL	

Thu

Description	Amount
TOTAL	

Weekly Expense Tracker

Total expenses :

Balance :

Fri

Description	Amount
TOTAL	

Sat

Description	Amount
TOTAL	

Sun

Description	Amount
TOTAL	

Notes

Monthly BUDGET

Month :

Budget :

Expenses

	Income	
Source1		
Source2		
Other Income		
TOTAL INCOME		

No.	Bill	Date	Amount	Paid
	TOTAL EXPENSES			

Monthly BUDGET

No.	Date	Other Expenses	Amount
		TOTAL OTHER EXPENSE	

Notes

TOTAL INCOME

TOTAL EXPENSES

DIFFERENCE

Weekly Expense Tracker

Month : **Week of :** **Budget :**

Mon

Description	Amount
TOTAL	

Tue

Description	Amount
TOTAL	

Wed

Description	Amount
TOTAL	

Thu

Description	Amount
TOTAL	

Weekly Expense Tracker

Total expenses :

Balance :

Fri

Description	Amount
TOTAL	

Sat

Description	Amount
TOTAL	

Sun

Description	Amount
TOTAL	

Notes

Weekly Expense Tracker

Month : **Week of :** **Budget :**

Mon

Description	Amount
TOTAL	

Tue

Description	Amount
TOTAL	

Wed

Description	Amount
TOTAL	

Thu

Description	Amount
TOTAL	

Weekly Expense Tracker

Total expenses :

Balance :

Fri

Description	Amount
TOTAL	

Sat

Description	Amount
TOTAL	

Sun

Description	Amount
TOTAL	

Notes

Weekly Expense Tracker

Month : **Week of :** **Budget :**

Mon

Description	Amount
TOTAL	

Tue

Description	Amount
TOTAL	

Wed

Description	Amount
TOTAL	

Thu

Description	Amount
TOTAL	

Weekly Expense Tracker

Total expenses :   **Balance :**

Fri

Description	Amount
TOTAL	

Sat

Description	Amount
TOTAL	

Sun

Description	Amount
TOTAL	

Notes

Weekly Expense Tracker

Month : **Week of :** **Budget :**

Mon

Description	Amount
TOTAL	

Tue

Description	Amount
TOTAL	

Wed

Description	Amount
TOTAL	

Thu

Description	Amount
TOTAL	

Weekly Expense Tracker

Total expenses :

Balance :

Fri

Description	Amount
TOTAL	

Sat

Description	Amount
TOTAL	

Sun

Description	Amount
TOTAL	

Notes

Weekly Expense Tracker

Month :   **Week of :**   **Budget :**

Mon

Description	Amount
TOTAL	

Tue

Description	Amount
TOTAL	

Wed

Description	Amount
TOTAL	

Thu

Description	Amount
TOTAL	

Weekly Expense Tracker

Total expenses :

Balance :

Fri

Description	Amount
TOTAL	

Sat

Description	Amount
TOTAL	

Sun

Description	Amount
TOTAL	

Notes

Monthly BUDGET

Month :

Budget :

Expenses

Income		
Source1		
Source2		
Other Income		
TOTAL INCOME		

No.	Bill	Date	Amount	Paid
	TOTAL EXPENSES			

Monthly BUDGET

No.	Date	Other Expenses	Amount
		TOTAL OTHER EXPENSE	

Notes

TOTAL INCOME

TOTAL EXPENSES

DIFFERENCE

Weekly Expense Tracker

Month :   **Week of :**   **Budget :**

Mon

Description	Amount
TOTAL	

Tue

Description	Amount
TOTAL	

Wed

Description	Amount
TOTAL	

Thu

Description	Amount
TOTAL	

Weekly Expense Tracker

Total expenses :

Balance :

Fri

Description	Amount
TOTAL	

Sat

Description	Amount
TOTAL	

Sun

Description	Amount
TOTAL	

Notes

Weekly Expense Tracker

Month :   **Week of :**   **Budget :**

Mon

Description	Amount
TOTAL	

Tue

Description	Amount
TOTAL	

Wed

Description	Amount
TOTAL	

Thu

Description	Amount
TOTAL	

Weekly Expense Tracker

Total expenses :

Balance :

Fri

Description	Amount
TOTAL	

Sat

Description	Amount
TOTAL	

Sun

Description	Amount
TOTAL	

Notes

Weekly Expense Tracker

Month :   **Week of :**   **Budget :**

Mon

Description	Amount
TOTAL	

Tue

Description	Amount
TOTAL	

Wed

Description	Amount
TOTAL	

Thu

Description	Amount
TOTAL	

Weekly Expense Tracker

Total expenses :

Balance :

Fri

Description	Amount
TOTAL	

Sat

Description	Amount
TOTAL	

Sun

Description	Amount
TOTAL	

Notes

Weekly Expense Tracker

Month : **Week of :** **Budget :**

Mon

Description	Amount
TOTAL	

Tue

Description	Amount
TOTAL	

Wed

Description	Amount
TOTAL	

Thu

Description	Amount
TOTAL	

Weekly Expense Tracker

Total expenses :

Balance :

Fri

Description	Amount
TOTAL	

Sat

Description	Amount
TOTAL	

Sun

Description	Amount
TOTAL	

Notes

Weekly Expense Tracker

Month :   **Week of :**   **Budget :**

Mon

Description	Amount
TOTAL	

Tue

Description	Amount
TOTAL	

Wed

Description	Amount
TOTAL	

Thu

Description	Amount
TOTAL	

Weekly Expense Tracker

Total expenses :

Balance :

Fri

Description	Amount
TOTAL	

Sat

Description	Amount
TOTAL	

Sun

Description	Amount
TOTAL	

Notes

Monthly BUDGET

Month :

Budget :

Expenses

Income		
Source1		
Source2		
Other Income		
TOTAL INCOME		

No.	Bill	Date	Amount	Paid
	TOTAL EXPENSES			

Monthly BUDGET

No.	Date	Other Expenses	Amount
		TOTAL OTHER EXPENSE	

Notes

TOTAL INCOME

TOTAL EXPENSES

DIFFERENCE

Weekly Expense Tracker

Month :   **Week of :**   **Budget :**

Mon

Description	Amount
TOTAL	

Tue

Description	Amount
TOTAL	

Wed

Description	Amount
TOTAL	

Thu

Description	Amount
TOTAL	

Weekly Expense Tracker

Total expenses : ▢   **Balance :** ▢

Fri

Description	Amount
TOTAL	

Sat

Description	Amount
TOTAL	

Sun

Description	Amount
TOTAL	

Notes

Weekly Expense Tracker

Month :   **Week of :**   **Budget :**

Mon

Description	Amount
TOTAL	

Tue

Description	Amount
TOTAL	

Wed

Description	Amount
TOTAL	

Thu

Description	Amount
TOTAL	

Weekly Expense Tracker

Total expenses :

Balance :

Fri

Description	Amount
TOTAL	

Sat

Description	Amount
TOTAL	

Sun

Description	Amount
TOTAL	

Notes

Weekly Expense Tracker

Month :   **Week of :**   **Budget :**

Mon

Description	Amount
TOTAL	

Tue

Description	Amount
TOTAL	

Wed

Description	Amount
TOTAL	

Thu

Description	Amount
TOTAL	

Weekly Expense Tracker

Total expenses :

Balance :

Fri

Description	Amount
TOTAL	

Sat

Description	Amount
TOTAL	

Sun

Description	Amount
TOTAL	

Notes

Weekly Expense Tracker

Month : _____   **Week of :** _____   **Budget :** _____

Mon

Description	Amount
TOTAL	

Tue

Description	Amount
TOTAL	

Wed

Description	Amount
TOTAL	

Thu

Description	Amount
TOTAL	

Weekly Expense Tracker

Total expenses :

Balance :

Fri

Description	Amount
TOTAL	

Sat

Description	Amount
TOTAL	

Sun

Description	Amount
TOTAL	

Notes

Weekly Expense Tracker

Month : _____   **Week of :** _____   **Budget :** _____

Mon

Description	Amount
TOTAL	

Tue

Description	Amount
TOTAL	

Wed

Description	Amount
TOTAL	

Thu

Description	Amount
TOTAL	

Weekly Expense Tracker

Total expenses :

Balance :

Fri

Description	Amount
TOTAL	

Sat

Description	Amount
TOTAL	

Sun

Description	Amount
TOTAL	

Notes

Monthly BUDGET

Month :

Budget :

Expenses

Income		
Source1		
Source2		
Other Income		
TOTAL INCOME		

No.	Bill	Date	Amount	Paid
	TOTAL EXPENSES			

Monthly BUDGET

No.	Date	Other Expenses	Amount
		TOTAL OTHER EXPENSE	

Notes

TOTAL INCOME

TOTAL EXPENSES

DIFFERENCE

Weekly Expense Tracker

Month :   **Week of :**   **Budget :**

Mon

Description	Amount
TOTAL	

Tue

Description	Amount
TOTAL	

Wed

Description	Amount
TOTAL	

Thu

Description	Amount
TOTAL	

Weekly Expense Tracker

Total expenses :

Balance :

Fri

Description	Amount
TOTAL	

Sat

Description	Amount
TOTAL	

Sun

Description	Amount
TOTAL	

Notes

Weekly Expense Tracker

Month :   **Week of :**   **Budget :**

Mon

Description	Amount
TOTAL	

Tue

Description	Amount
TOTAL	

Wed

Description	Amount
TOTAL	

Thu

Description	Amount
TOTAL	

Weekly Expense Tracker

Total expenses :

Balance :

Fri

Description	Amount
TOTAL	

Sat

Description	Amount
TOTAL	

Sun

Description	Amount
TOTAL	

Notes

Weekly Expense Tracker

Month : _____   **Week of :** _____   **Budget :** _____

Mon

Description	Amount
TOTAL	

Tue

Description	Amount
TOTAL	

Wed

Description	Amount
TOTAL	

Thu

Description	Amount
TOTAL	

Weekly Expense Tracker

Total expenses :

Balance :

Fri

Description	Amount
TOTAL	

Sat

Description	Amount
TOTAL	

Sun

Description	Amount
TOTAL	

Notes

Weekly Expense Tracker

Month :　　　　　　　　**Week of :**　　　　　**Budget :**

Mon

Description	Amount
TOTAL	

Tue

Description	Amount
TOTAL	

Wed

Description	Amount
TOTAL	

Thu

Description	Amount
TOTAL	

Weekly Expense Tracker

Total expenses :

Balance :

Fri

Description	Amount
TOTAL	

Sat

Description	Amount
TOTAL	

Sun

Description	Amount
TOTAL	

Notes

Weekly Expense Tracker

Month :   **Week of :**   **Budget :**

Mon

Description	Amount
TOTAL	

Tue

Description	Amount
TOTAL	

Wed

Description	Amount
TOTAL	

Thu

Description	Amount
TOTAL	

Weekly Expense Tracker

Total expenses :

Balance :

Fri

Description	Amount
TOTAL	

Sat

Description	Amount
TOTAL	

Sun

Description	Amount
TOTAL	

Notes

Monthly BUDGET

Month :

Budget :

Expenses

Income		
Source1		
Source2		
Other Income		
TOTAL INCOME		

No.	Bill	Date	Amount	Paid
		TOTAL EXPENSES		

Monthly BUDGET

No.	Date	Other Expenses	Amount
		TOTAL OTHER EXPENSE	

Notes

TOTAL INCOME

TOTAL EXPENSES

DIFFERENCE

Weekly Expense Tracker

Month : **Week of :** **Budget :**

Mon

Description	Amount
TOTAL	

Tue

Description	Amount
TOTAL	

Wed

Description	Amount
TOTAL	

Thu

Description	Amount
TOTAL	

Weekly Expense Tracker

Total expenses :

Balance :

Fri

Description	Amount
TOTAL	

Sat

Description	Amount
TOTAL	

Sun

Description	Amount
TOTAL	

Notes

Weekly Expense Tracker

Month : **Week of :** **Budget :**

Mon

Description	Amount
TOTAL	

Tue

Description	Amount
TOTAL	

Wed

Description	Amount
TOTAL	

Thu

Description	Amount
TOTAL	

Weekly Expense Tracker

Total expenses :

Balance :

Fri

Description	Amount
TOTAL	

Sat

Description	Amount
TOTAL	

Sun

Description	Amount
TOTAL	

Notes

Weekly Expense Tracker

Month : **Week of :** **Budget :**

Mon

Description	Amount
TOTAL	

Tue

Description	Amount
TOTAL	

Wed

Description	Amount
TOTAL	

Thu

Description	Amount
TOTAL	

Weekly Expense Tracker

Total expenses :

Balance :

Fri

Description	Amount
TOTAL	

Sat

Description	Amount
TOTAL	

Sun

Description	Amount
TOTAL	

Notes

Weekly Expense Tracker

Month :   **Week of :**   **Budget :**

Mon

Description	Amount
TOTAL	

Tue

Description	Amount
TOTAL	

Wed

Description	Amount
TOTAL	

Thu

Description	Amount
TOTAL	

Weekly Expense Tracker

Total expenses :

Balance :

Fri

Description	Amount
TOTAL	

Sat

Description	Amount
TOTAL	

Sun

Description	Amount
TOTAL	

Notes

Weekly Expense Tracker

Month : _____   **Week of :** _____   **Budget :** _____

Mon

Description	Amount
TOTAL	

Tue

Description	Amount
TOTAL	

Wed

Description	Amount
TOTAL	

Thu

Description	Amount
TOTAL	

Weekly Expense Tracker

Total expenses :

Balance :

Fri

Description	Amount
TOTAL	

Sat

Description	Amount
TOTAL	

Sun

Description	Amount
TOTAL	

Notes

Monthly BUDGET

Month :

Budget :

Expenses

Income		
Source1		
Source2		
Other Income		
TOTAL INCOME		

No.	Bill	Date	Amount	Paid
		TOTAL EXPENSES		

Monthly BUDGET

No.	Date	Other Expenses	Amount
		TOTAL OTHER EXPENSE	

Notes

TOTAL INCOME

TOTAL EXPENSES

DIFFERENCE

Weekly Expense Tracker

Month : _____ **Week of :** _____ **Budget :** _____

Mon

Description	Amount
TOTAL	

Tue

Description	Amount
TOTAL	

Wed

Description	Amount
TOTAL	

Thu

Description	Amount
TOTAL	

Weekly Expense Tracker

Total expenses :

Balance :

Fri

Description	Amount
TOTAL	

Sat

Description	Amount
TOTAL	

Sun

Description	Amount
TOTAL	

Notes

Weekly Expense Tracker

Month :   **Week of :**   **Budget :**

Mon

Description	Amount
TOTAL	

Tue

Description	Amount
TOTAL	

Wed

Description	Amount
TOTAL	

Thu

Description	Amount
TOTAL	

Weekly Expense Tracker

Total expenses :

Balance :

Fri

Description	Amount
TOTAL	

Sat

Description	Amount
TOTAL	

Sun

Description	Amount
TOTAL	

Notes

Weekly Expense Tracker

Month :   **Week of :**   **Budget :**

Mon

Description	Amount
TOTAL	

Tue

Description	Amount
TOTAL	

Wed

Description	Amount
TOTAL	

Thu

Description	Amount
TOTAL	

Weekly Expense Tracker

Total expenses :   **Balance :**

Fri

Description	Amount
TOTAL	

Sat

Description	Amount
TOTAL	

Sun

Description	Amount
TOTAL	

Notes

Weekly Expense Tracker

Month :　　　　　　　　　**Week of :**　　　　**Budget :**

Mon

Description	Amount
TOTAL	

Tue

Description	Amount
TOTAL	

Wed

Description	Amount
TOTAL	

Thu

Description	Amount
TOTAL	

Weekly Expense Tracker

Total expenses :

Balance :

Fri

Description	Amount
TOTAL	

Sat

Description	Amount
TOTAL	

Sun

Description	Amount
TOTAL	

Notes

Weekly Expense Tracker

Month : **Week of :** **Budget :**

Mon

Description	Amount
TOTAL	

Tue

Description	Amount
TOTAL	

Wed

Description	Amount
TOTAL	

Thu

Description	Amount
TOTAL	

Weekly Expense Tracker

Total expenses :

Balance :

Fri

Description	Amount
TOTAL	

Sat

Description	Amount
TOTAL	

Sun

Description	Amount
TOTAL	

Notes

Notes

CPSIA information can be obtained
at www.ICGtesting.com
Printed in the USA
LVHW02s1105051018
592514LV00003B/4/P